EMBODIED
CONFIDENCE

EMBODIED CONFIDENCE

30 DAYS OF
RADICAL
MINDSET SHIFTS
for CHEERLEADERS

SARA VATORE

SOMASYNTHESIS PRESS

ISBN: 978-1-955789-04-2 (paperback)
ISBN: 978-1-955789-05-9 (ebook)

Somasynthesis Press
www.saravatore.com

For all the inspiring, passionate cheerleaders
I have worked with and learned from
over the years. Thank you!

Introduction

Did you know that feeling CONFIDENT as a cheerleader is possible?

Hi there! I'm Sara and I'm a Peak Performance Coach.

I come across too many cheerleaders who worry that their fears and self doubts are unusual, believing they're the only one experiencing these thoughts and feelings!

I'm here to set the record straight and give you a roadmap to consistently experience more confidence in your training and performance.

You see, it's NORMAL for ALL cheerleaders to feel scared, frightened, and nervous to do particular skills at some point or another.

It's also NORMAL for ALL cheerleaders to compare themselves to others, worry about hitting their routine at a competition, or wonder if they'll ever get to move up to the next level.

I get it. You want to do a good job. You won't stop at anything short of perfect to meet your goals.

And yet, do you find yourself frustrated when you make mistakes or have a bad day at practice? You try so hard, but still don't feel consistently confident and secure in yourself or your training?

As someone who has spent over 1000 hours in the gym observing and working with cheerleaders, gymnasts and coaches, I've heard hundreds of the same kinds of stories:

Cheerleaders who:

- wish they felt more confident

- deal with persistent negative thinking and self doubts.

- wish they knew what to do about feeling scared to go for a new skill.

- get so frustrated at themselves for making mistakes.

- would love to get consistent with their routines.

- have "lost skills" or feel blocked on skills they've been able to do for years.

- constantly compare themselves to their teammates or opponents.

- want to easily calm themselves down before a competition.

After working with hundreds of gymnasts and cheerleaders in and out of the gym it's clear there's BASIC information missing from foundational cheer education about how our brain and body work, and how this influences athletic performance.

Fortunately, you can learn how to help your body feel confident! This is a skill, just like learning a back handspring or stunts.

You can train your brain to think differently! How would it feel to reduce those negative thoughts and doubts?

There are simple concepts, practices, and tools you can learn and practice to make you feel more confident, consistent and an overall better athlete TODAY!

I wrote this book because every cheerleader should have these foundational pieces of mind-body-performance information to make their cheer training and competition execution easier, more focused, and more consistent.

Being a cheerleader is hard work. You have to put in the time and effort to excel in this sport. It's physically and mentally demanding, time consuming and requires a certain level of grit.

You devote hundreds of hours physically practicing. It's also necessary to dedicate yourself to training the mental side of your sport. When it's your turn at the next competition, you don't want to leave this all important aspect of your performance to chance!

This book is designed to help you understand what cheerleaders do mentally that prevent them from achieving peak performance.

At the same time, you'll begin to understand your body and how it communicates to you, in order to maximize your body's potential and truly execute like a champion when it counts.

As you read this book, you'll build a new awareness about your mindset and your body. You'll see how to integrate these exercises and tools into your training so you can move through fear and blocks with more ease and embody your most confident self!

What is EMBODIMENT?

EMBODIMENT is your self- perception and experience of BEING in your own body.

When you're embodied, you can SENSE your body, feel your body connected in your environment, and precisely identify physically what's happening inside your body (for example, your heart beat, breath or tightening muscles).

Our bodies are our greatest teachers. They communicate information to us, are wired to protect us, and often operate completely out of our awareness.

They are responsible for our ability to live and breathe in this world as a human!

While it's VERY common in the peak performance communities to discuss MINDSET and how to make mental toughness shifts, this book offers an additional perspective and orientation focused on the body that can unlock your full cheer potential.

As a cheerleader your body is at the core of everything you do. It's what you're training and programming to execute specific skills, stunts and routines.

In school we aren't taught much about our bodies and our physiological wiring. In fact, academic settings often keep us stuck in our heads and caught up in our thinking. In general, we aren't paying attention to our body's messages or signals unless there's something significantly wrong, like pain or illness.

Being in your body, being able to sense your body, and specifically being able to sense your body in the environments and spaces you're in, is KEY to accessing your ultimate potential as a cheerleader. It also helps you thrive in your day to day experience.

Your active awareness of your EMBODIMENT is essential to make long lasting change and is the secret ingredient to ULTIMATE PEAK PERFOR-MANCE.

Especially as a cheerleader, your awareness of your body, being able to sense the movement shapes and patterns you make (your choreo!), is essential for executing precise stunts and skills. This is also how you become attuned at sensing what needs to be adjusted with your body when you make a mistake during practice or at a competition.

Think about it, having the ability to sense in your body what corrections you need without a coach telling you?! Why that IS a SUPERPOWER!

The reason you practice your routines, tumbling and stunts over and over is because you're creating embodiment patterns in your whole system. This way your body automatically remembers what it needs to do once you get to that big competition.

You can try to make all the mindset shifts you want, but if you can't deeply feel the changes in your body, you're at a disadvantage. They just won't stick!

Embodying CONFIDENCE and the other ways you want to feel as a cheerleader (focused, determined, fluid, relaxed, joyful), in addition to mind-set shifts, is the formula for expanding your capacity and accessing success.

We need to move beyond just valuing the brain and our thinking. Your body is a gateway to excellence, so EMBODIMENT (increasing your ability to be in and sense your body) is how you gain an extra edge on your competitors. This is what allows you to become a champion with the greatest confidence and ease!

SENSATIONS Explained

In order to understand EMBODIMENT completely, we have to talk about SENSATIONS.

We are most familiar with using our thinking minds and don't focus on the body as much, unless there's a major issue, like injury or illness. This book invites you to understand your body in a more expansive way.

The language of the body is sensation. Sensations are the internal experiences inside your body, like your heartbeat, muscle twitching or butterflies in your stomach.

Sensations give you information about what your body needs and what your truth is in the moment.

When you start to pay attention to your body, it can be challenging. You might not notice very much at first. You may also not have the language to describe your sensations yet.

This is perfectly normal! Be patient with yourself. You're learning a new language, which takes time and practice. The more you observe, the easier it becomes to sense your body and expand your vocabulary to describe your sensations.

Some examples of sensations:

Calm, warm, heavy, jittery, tense,
frozen, stuck, clammy, hot, sparkly,
light, long, hollow

You can start practicing this right now with these simple questions:

- What sensations do you notice right now in your body?

- How would you describe them?

The more you observe (and name) your sensations, the easier it is to notice them automatically!

What is EMBODIED CONFIDENCE?

Think back to a time in your life where you experienced feeling confident, like that first time you stuck your roundoff back handspring tuck or when your team placed 1st in a competition. It can be a memory from cheer or another environment, like school or hanging out with friends.

Bring that image in your mind.

- What did it feel like in your body at that moment? What SENSATIONS did you experience?

- What did you notice about being CONFIDENT?

If you want to feel CONFIDENT you have to know what CONFIDENCE feels like in your body.

When you're confident, your body feels a certain way. When I'm confident I feel my feet rooted and connected to the ground. I sense length in my spine and back, my shoulders are relaxed and lowered, I can look out and around at the world, and I feel loose in my whole body.

Confidence FEELS a certain way for each of us in our body. Your experience of confidence will feel unique to you.

We each have our own embodiment pattern of CONFIDENCE. When you know what those specific sensations are for your body, you can easily find this pattern when you need it, like at a competition.

EMBODIED CONFIDENCE is when your thoughts of "I am confident" align with how your body feels inside and what your body looks like on the outside. You sense confidence within and throughout your whole body.

Setting the foundation

As you dive into this book, there are a few foundational mindset shifts that will allow you to get the most of these invitations:

- **Maintain a beginner's mind as you read**

The concepts in this book will be a mix of new concepts and things you've heard of before. Keeping an open mind, also called a beginner's mind, is the most effective way to take as much of the information into your brain and body as possible. Beginners are CURIOUS and when we can be curious, we are most receptive to learning and making changes!

- **Approach reading and learning with the spirit of CURIOSITY**

Curiosity keeps us open and receptive to learning new things and allows these ideas to process in our minds. When we are learning new things, we may be judgmental. You may direct the judgment towards yourself ("I should've known that!) or towards the material ("That is never going to work").

A judgmental mindset closes our system down and prevents our brain from being available for new learning.

The more you can stay curious about yourself, your observations and your thoughts, the more you'll get out of this book.

• **To create long lasting changes, mindset shifts, and embodied confidence, read this book and practice the exercises multiple times.**

Change requires commitment and hard work. This book was written as a tool you can come back to again and again. Each time you read a chapter, you may have a new learning or make a new observation. To get the most out of the material, teachings and affirmations, it requires you to choose to practice and work with them on a regular basis.

Learning a new skill in the gym requires repetition, and lots of it! This is why you practice your routines over and over again, as a way for your brain and body to develop muscle memory (to be able to remember the pattern). This is the same for mindset and embodiment work. Practice leads to lasting shifts!

Understanding affirmations and how to use them

You'll notice that each chapter has an affirmation sentence that corresponds with the theme for that day. Affirmations are present moment statements that help us shape our thinking and brain to begin to generate new beliefs.

We tend to believe what we think because our thoughts influence our state of being. In other words, our thinking affects how we feel in our body. If you have a lot of negative thoughts and a pattern of thinking more negatively about yourself and situations in your life, it can make you feel pretty crummy inside. This is because our body begins to believe we are those negative things.

The good news is that we can use the power of our minds to create new beliefs and feeling states in our bodies! Isn't that amazing? Working with affirmations is a way to effectively reprogram our thinking patterns.

You can use affirmations to shape and strengthen your mind and train your brain to think in a different way. You can work with them to help find your motivation, increase your self esteem, and encourage the positive changes you would like to see in your behavior!

How to work with an affirmation:

There is no one "right" way to work with affirmations. The more you repeat them to yourself, the more your body will start to believe the statements to be true. For effective and lasting change, it takes a personal commitment to regularly practice with them!

Below are some possibilities for working with affirmations. Try them out and see what feels most helpful for you. Get creative and try something that's not on the list!

1. Put the affirmation statement up on your wall in your room, in a place you look at often, like by your computer or mirror. Repeat it out loud or to yourself every time you walk by.

2. Repeat the affirmation out loud or in your head 5-10 times as you are getting ready in the morning, before practice or before you go to bed (or all of the above).

3. Set an alarm to go off throughout your day with the affirmation written in the notes, so it flashes on your phone alerts.

4. During conditioning or at other in-between spaces at gym (while you are waiting for your turn or having a break) repeat the affirmation to yourself in your head.

5. Allow the affirmation to be your default thought for the day. Every time you notice you're thinking or stressing about something, catch yourself, bring your attention back to yourself, and repeat the affirmation.

6. Pair a visualization with your affirmation statement. If you're working with the statement *"I am calm, relaxed and confident"*, remember a time and picture yourself, in your mind's eye, when you felt really calm, relaxed and confident.

7. Write the affirmation statement down in your journal multiple times. Speak it out loud as you write.

How to work with this book

There are a few different ways to read and work with this book. Every chapter has an affirmation statement, a short explanation and teaching nugget, followed by a practice invitation. There is no "right" way to read through the chapters.

See below for some possibilities and ask yourself what would be most fun or helpful for you right now!

Read one chapter per day for 30 days

Make a commitment to read one entire chapter first thing in the morning each day for 30 days and follow the instructions for the daily practice. Journal at night what you observed. You can start at the beginning of a month, or at any time.

Work with one affirmation statement every day for 30 days

You can start at the beginning of a month, or at any time. Make a commitment to read the same affirmation statement each day for 30 days. Focus on and repeat that individual affirmation throughout each day. Reflect at night in your journal what you notice about how you feel about yourself, cheer and your mindset.

Flip the book open to a random page and read the chapter

Sometimes we need some guidance, but we aren't sure what would be helpful. If you need inspiration at any time, whether it's at home, before a practice or during a meet, pick up the book and flip it open to a random page. Read the chapter and see what message is available for you. Follow through on the practice invitation for more guidance and reflection.

Go and look for the inspiration you need the most

We all have those harder days when we need a little pick-me-up. If you're struggling with a particular concept or challenge at practice, flip through the book and find the chapter that could be the most helpful for you to read at that moment. Work with the affirmation throughout the day and the invitation for observation and practice.

Work with one concept each week

Each chapter has the potential to be its own longer exploration and awareness building experience. Make a commitment to read one chapter at the beginning of a week. Then observe and reflect on that theme throughout the unfolding week, both in your life and at the gym. On a daily basis, work with the affirmation statement and practice invitations. Journal throughout the week to track your expanding observations. When the next week begins, choose another chapter to play with and focus on.

No matter how you choose to work with this book, I recommend keeping all your reflections in one journal. This is a helpful way to see your new awareness and observations of your embodied confidence unfold all in one space!

I

This is a judgement free zone

How you speak to yourself inside your head matters!

How you respond to what is happening around you affects how you feel inside your body.

What gets in the way too often for cheerleaders is their own SELF JUDGEMENT and internal criticism. This usually looks like having an opinion and story about everything that is happening.

They are stressed out about WHY something is happening (or not happening).

- "Why am I not going?"

- "Why is my body not going?"

- "Why can't we get our new routine down?"

- "Why can't I get this skill today, I was able to do it yesterday?"

- "Why do I feel this way? I shouldn't feel like this."

So many cheerleaders judge everything that's happening or get upset about what they THINK is happening. They label everything good, bad or very bad! There are things that "should be" happening and things that "shouldn't be" happening.

All this judgement causes unnecessary performance problems.

Judgement creates the feelings of pressure and urgency inside our bodies.

Want to know a trick to avoid adding more stress and doubt in your practices and at your competitions?

Get NEUTRAL with yourself and your observations!

What does neutral mean?

Neutral means staying non-judgmental. It looks like not having an opinion about your mistakes, feelings, performance, or thoughts. It's not spiraling in your thinking.

It's naming what is happening and moving on with your cheer skills, like:

- "Oh, my body is not letting me throw my backhandspring."

- "My new routine is challenging today. I can work more on things tomorrow."

- "I was able to go for my standing tuck yesterday. Today feels harder."

- "I feel really frustrated today."

The more neutral you can be about what you're observing (your thoughts, feelings, emotions, and performance), the easier it is to let things go, not hook into hyper focusing on your thoughts and access your most confident cheer self!

INVITATION & PRACTICE

Identify and Practice: At practice work on becoming a NEUTRAL OBSERVER.

A NEUTRAL OBSERVER is able to witness what's happening inside of you (your thoughts, sensations, and feelings) and what is happening around you (the environment, other people) without JUDGE-MENT or an OPINION.

If you notice a judgmental thought, gently allow your attention to come back to yourself, and let the thought pass, without hooking into your judgement.

Write down your observations in your journal after practice about what you noticed.

Finding your NEUTRAL OBSERVER is a foundational skill to become the most focused and confident cheerleader you can be as you build your awareness throughout the rest of this book!

Continually return to this practice.

2

My awareness
gives me choice

You can't become a champion without training your mind as well as your body.

There's a lot happening inside our bodies and minds automatically, outside of our awareness, which affects our performance and execution of skills.

Especially when we're working hard towards something we care about and we're driven towards a goal, we can get influenced and affected by our mindset, whether it's positive or negative.

When your thinking turns negative, it greatly impacts your body during training and competition.

You might think spiraling in your negative thinking and self doubts is just the way that it is. As a flyer you might think you'll always be terrified of your toe touch basket and will never do it. You might think you're destined to perform better in practice than at your competitions forever.

You can't make any changes or improve your mindset unless you understand and recognize what you're doing in the first place.

You can't know what you don't know.

So your first step to excellence is to build SELF AWARENESS.

When you're aware of YOU, what's happening in YOUR mind, in YOUR body, and in the environment around YOU, there's an opportunity for CHOICE.

When you recognize you have a CHOICE, you can make a CHANGE to do something differently.

Our bodies and minds are WIRED for change.

This is excellent news.
You aren't stuck in any one way.
Your SELF AWARENESS is the key to this change.

INVITATION & PRACTICE

Reflection: Imagine someone gives you a magic wand that could change anything instantly about what's happening for you at practices and competitions (your fears, self talk, thinking, confidence level).

- What would you change?
- What do you want to be different?

Write your answers down in your journal.

Observation: Begin to observe all your negative thoughts over the course of the day, in and out of the gym, related or unrelated to your cheerleading. You don't need to remember exactly what you said, just assign a number to every negative thing that pops up.

Just the process of recognizing these negative thoughts and counting them, without engaging in them, will help you begin to reduce them!

Comparison thoughts like, "*She's so much stronger than me,*" or "*She's so much better, I'll never be that good*" are all negative. Remember, we can't make a change, if we aren't aware of what we're doing in the first place.

This awareness expansion is the very first step to beginning to turn things around!

3

I listen to my body,
I honor my body's needs

All day long our bodies are communicating important information to us. They're intelligent organisms and know exactly what we need in order to survive!

From hunger cues when we need food, to pain when we hurt ourselves, from heaviness when we're sad, to a fast heartbeat when we're nervous, every sensation in the body is a message about our personal truth in the moment.

However, we aren't taught how to listen to our body! It communicates to us in a very specific way: through the sensations we feel on the inside.

We often don't know how to interpret these sensations. We either freak out about them (like when you feel your heart rate beating out of your chest before a competition starts), OR we're totally unaware they're happening inside us at all.

Sometimes you are aware when you're ignoring your body's messages, like if a coach is yelling at you and you make a choice to swallow your tears to put on a brave face. Other times, you aren't even aware your body is sending you a message in the first place.

However, if your needs aren't being met, your body will give you louder clues that something is up.

Without enough sleep, rest, nourishing foods and plenty of water, your body will feel tired and heavy. You'll have a harder time pulling yourself together to be motivated and push it in your workouts.

What might happen if you shrug off the fact that your foot is hurting and you continue training on it for weeks? By ignoring this discomfort, you could develop a long term injury.

If you don't let yourself feel anger and continue to stuff it down and ignore it, you'll feel heavier in your body and unsettled day to day, which will affect your training.

When you ignore the early sensations from your body, it gets louder until you have no choice but to listen.

This is an invitation to
begin to listen NOW.

By honoring what your body is asking for, in and out of the gym, you can feel dramatically better in your life. You will be inspired to follow through on your passions and have energy to work towards your goals!

INVITATION & PRACTICE

Reflection and observation: We have to know what it feels like when our body is communicating to us so we know how to listen. This starts with checking in with your body regularly and beginning to honor the basic information that your system is telling you. Notice today:

- Are you hungry?
- Do you have to use the bathroom?
- Do you need a minute to let yourself feel frustrated?
- Are you tired and need a break?

Give yourself permission to slow down and ask yourself throughout the day: what do I need right now?

Listen to the answers! Journal your thoughts about what you discover.

4

I believe in myself

What does the internal chatter in your head at practice sound like? What are you thinking about? Did you know all cheerleaders have some sort of internal thinking going on throughout practice?!

Whether you're thinking about your upcoming homework, the mistakes you made on your tumbling, or comparing yourself to your teammates, this kind of thinking takes your focus away from the primary task at hand: your cheerleading.

When things go wrong at practice, our internal chatter easily turns negative and out comes our Inner Critic.

Instead of focusing on that unhelpful voice, how can you hear and connect with your True Inner Coach?

This is the part of you who is a positive, supportive coach who ALWAYS knows the right thing to say to motivate you.

No matter what kind of practice or competition is happening, your True Inner Coach does not yell at you, call you names or make you feel badly about yourself or your skills.

Your True Inner Coach BELIEVES IN YOU every moment and every day.

They are your encouraging inner cheerleader.

It's time to get your True Inner Coach front and center. Invite them to come to each practice and competition so your inner dialogue helps you feel good about yourself and your skills! This will support you to execute your stunts and routines with more consistency and confidence.

INVITATION & PRACTICE

Observation: As practice begins today, Invite your True Inner Coach to join you. (You can even give them a name, like "Motivational Mindy").

Journal after practice:

- What kind of inner coach were you to yourself today?
- What did you say to yourself that lets you know?
- Write down what you discover in your journal.

Journal Practice: Keep a CELEBRATIONS LOG in your journal. Every day write down at least 5 small "celebrations". They can be cheer related or not.

You can include things that teachers and coaches have said to you, experiences you are proud of, like moving toward an obstacle or fear, or anything else, like a newspaper clipping or image from a magazine that represents something from gym or school.

5

I am excited and motivated by my dreams

If you want to be exceptional as a cheerleader, you need a clear DREAM or reason WHY you're doing it in the first place! A dream gives you the focus you need to work hard and make the sacrifices that go into being a competitive cheer athlete.

I call this dream your BIG WHY.

When you have a powerful BIG WHY, it becomes the MOTIVATION behind all of your hard work. Your dreams help drive your effort and they get you training hard and focused at gym!

- Why are you training in the first place?

- Why are you putting in all that time at practice?

- What lights you up about cheer?

Motivation is something that comes from deep within YOURSELF, an inner fire that rises up within you. Revisit the reasons you began cheerleading in the first place and let them MOVE and EXCITE you.

What about cheer brings you joy? When we experience joy and pleasure from something, we're more likely to want to do it again and again.

You want to make sure your BIG WHY comes from within you and is not about pleasing your parents, friends and coaches or making them happy. You should NOT be doing cheer for your parents or anyone else except YOU!

Cheerleading is HARD WORK. If you're not training for yourself, it's going to be difficult to push through challenging moments, big obstacles and really give it your all.

When your desire and passion for cheer comes from within YOU, that is where the POWER lies. Your vibrant energy and determination can emerge fueling your motivation!

Anything you dream of or believe in,
you can achieve!

You have the power to create your own reality! You
have a powerful mind and body, so when you direct
your energy and focus towards your BIG WHY or
DREAM, it will attract like a magnet!

INVITATION & PRACTICE

Reflection: Brainstorm and write about your BIG WHY in your journal. Find something or make something to represent this DREAM visually to have in your room for inspiration.

You can cut out pictures from cheer magazines and make a collage, get a big poster of your favorite college cheerleader to put up on your door, or do something different.

Use this creative visual as daily motivation to help remind you of your WHY!

6

I focus on the FEEL of my body DOING my skills.

(I focus on FEEL)

It's so easy for cheerleaders to get caught up in their thoughts during practice and at competitions! But overthinking affects your performance and ability to execute your cheer skills, and not in a good way!

Instead of automatically thinking, we want to train our brain to focus on the right stuff.

What does that mean for a cheerleader? If your attention is not on your thoughts, what is the right stuff for you to focus on?

You want to concentrate on the FEEL: the FEEL of your body DOING the cheer skills and the sensations of your body making your shapes as you execute choreography.

Every skill in cheer has a
just-right-feel in your body.

Every routine has a specific flow and rhythm in your body when you're doing it well.

You can learn how to focus your attention on the FEEL of what you're DOING with your body instead of on the thoughts in your head!

Some examples of where to put your attention when you FOCUS ON FEEL:

1. **Doing a handstand:** I sense my hands pressing into the floor, the squeeze of my legs together, and the tightness in my core.

2. **When stretching:** I notice the pulling sensation in the back of my legs, the stretch and lengthening in my arms reaching out and I sense my butt connecting on the floor.

3. **When walking:** I sense my feet connected to the floor, I feel my arms swinging, and sense

the rhythm of my steps.

4. **When washing the dishes:** I sense the temperature of the water on my hands. I feel the weight of the dish I am washing. I can feel the texture of the bubbles from the soap on my fingers.

5. **When falling asleep:** I sense the softness of my mattress, the smoothness of the pillowcase and slight pressure from the weight of the covers on my body.

INVITATION & PRACTICE

Today at practice: Hold the intention to FOCUS ON FEEL at practice. Sense your body in every shape you make and each skill and stunt you execute. Notice your feet as you transition events. If you notice your attention goes back to your thinking, not to worry!

Gently bring your attention back to the FEEL of your body DOING your skills and routines.

Record your observations in your journal after practice.

7

I sense my feet on the ground
and my body in the space.
This is my NOW MOMENT.

We do our best cheerleading when we concentrate on BEING in the NOW MOMENT.

What is the NOW MOMENT?

The NOW MOMENT is when my attention is on what my body is DOING in the present time.

I'm not focusing on my thoughts about what has happened in the past, or what's coming up in the future. I'm not thinking about my teammates, coaches, parents, judges or any other people in my life. I'm not worrying about all the things I can't control, like if I slept well the night before the big competition or if my coach is in a bad mood at practice.

Instead, in the NOW MOMENT, I concentrate on the FEEL of my body in the space around me and the internal SENSATIONS inside my body, like my breath or my heart beat.

You do your best tumbling and cheerleading when you're in your NOW MOMENT. This is where you're sensing your body DOING each skill and stunt. You're focused on the FEEL of your body making the shapes of every element.

To practice being in the NOW MOMENT at the gym, focus on sensing the shapes your body is making while you're doing your routine or tumbling.

You want to keep your attention focused on the FEEL of your body during practices and at competitions, instead of on the THOUGHTS in your head.

INVITATION & PRACTICE

Today at school or home: Practice coming back into your NOW MOMENT. Pick one block of time during the day to practice this awareness, like a meal time, during classes at school, or at practice. When you notice that you're thinking, bring your attention back to where your feet connect to the floor or sense what your body is DOING in the space in that very moment.

Reflect on practicing coming back into your NOW MOMENT:

- Did you find you spent a lot of time thinking during this block of time?

- What did you notice about practicing coming back into your NOW MOMENT?

- Are some times during the day easier than others to focus on your NOW MOMENT?

Remember, no judgement! The more awareness we have of the way our body and brain works, the more changes we can make. Write down your observations in your journal at night.

8

I am centered and focused

How many times have you been told by your coach to just "FOCUS!" while you're at practice? What does that actually mean? How do you get there?

To do your best cheerleading, you must be able to stay centered and focused on the right stuff. We do our best focusing when our body is calm and in a neutral state.

I call this place, the BASELINE.

Your BASELINE is your foundation. It's the resting place for your body. It's your state of being (how your body feels) when you're grounded, connected, centered and ready to execute a skill.

The BASELINE is where our body returns to after we feel a big emotion, like stepping out of our comfort zone, having a scary close call as a flyer, or getting into an argument with a teammate.

By building awareness of what your BASELINE sensation feels like in your body, you have something very familiar to return to when you're thrown off during practice or when your body gets spooked from working on a certain skill.

If this BASELINE is not a place your body is used to, it's very challenging to bring your body there when you're having a hard time at practice or at a competition and just want to calm down.

Cheerleading is a sport that sometimes triggers fear in our bodies. As mammals, we were not designed to twist and flip upside down or get tossed up in the air and then land on our feet! Doing new skills or executing skills where we have hurt ourselves or seen someone else hurt themselves in the past, can be scary to the part of our body that's designed to keep us safe: our nervous system.

Because of this, at practice or competitions, you may find yourself super nervous to do things or struggling with skills you used to be able to do easily.

To move through these hard times, the very first step is to build a powerful awareness of what it feels like in your body when you're at your BASE-LINE.

INVITATION & PRACTICE

Journal Reflection: We are going to use a concept called **The Activation Scale**, to measure and observe our activation. On a scale of 0 to 10, where 10 is highly ACTIVATED (my body is worried, angry, fearful, stressed, frustrated, upset, excited) and 0 is my BASELINE, (my body is calm, relaxed, and centered), ask yourself:

- Where and when am I a zero? Are you hanging out with friends? Is it Sunday morning and you don't have to get up for school? Is it at the beach on vacation? Is it something different?

- Begin to brainstorm a list of all the times you're a zero day to day and where you are. What did it feel like in your body during those times?

What sensations do you notice
when you're at your BASELINE?

- Keep notes in your journal about
  what you discover.

9

My thoughts are not facts

———————————

Did you know your thoughts aren't true, that they're not actual facts?

Think about that for a moment.

Your thoughts are simply brain-wave activity.

We often respond to our own thoughts like they're the absolute truth. Then, we get so upset about the thoughts (and have more thoughts about these thoughts) because we believe they are true.

Now, we're making up an entire story around the original thought, spiraling into confusion and getting upset with and at ourselves!

Most of us have an internal voice that can be super negative. It might feel like a mean Inner Coach cracking the whip, yelling inside of your head-faster, better, stronger.

I call this, the CRITIC or the BOSS. This is the little voice (or loud one) that says you're a horrible cheerleader today and you'll never get the skill. It's the voice that compares you to your teammates or opponents.

You can learn how to stop listening to and believing this part of yourself, so it's no longer running the show in your brain. You can learn how to allow the thoughts to pass through, so you can easily observe them and let them go.

Your thoughts have a huge impact on how you feel in your physical body.

If you have a negative thought about yourself during practice, like "I'm never going to get this!", you'll have an upset feeling inside your body that matches that thought, which can easily tank your performance that day.

The trick is to begin noticing when your Inner Critic or Negative Coach comes out, so you can interrupt those thoughts!

You'd never speak to a teammate or best friend the way you sometimes talk to yourself. Start right now by being a supportive and positive coach to yourself and you'll find your self-confidence, motivation, and belief in yourself growing.

INVITATION & PRACTICE

Name your Inner Critic: Sometimes it's easier to identify when your Inner Critic or Inner Negative Coach comes out when you give them a funny name. It can break up some of the tension of your negative thoughts when you recognize them coming from more of a character rather than your true self.

A few of my favorite Inner Critic names from my cheer athletes are: Negative Nancy, Doofenshmirtz (from Phineas and Ferb), Critic, and Frownie Franie.

Today at practice: Notice when your Inner Critic comes out with their unhelpful opinion of you or your skills. If they do, gently refocus your attention on the FEEL of what you're DOING in your body in your NOW MOMENT with your skills. Repeat as necessary. Journal when you get home about what you noticed.

10

My choice point brings me back into my NOW MOMENT

———————

Cheerleaders think a lot! Your attention and focus can drift so many times during practice and even during competitions to all sorts of things. You may find yourself thinking about the rival team, the skills you need to get for tryouts, wondering why your teammate is getting their tumbling down faster than you, the homework you have left to do, or even what you'll be having for dinner.

While this is totally normal, we want to train our brain to stay focused in the NOW MOMENT on the FEEL of what we are DOING at the gym.

When we concentrate on our thoughts, we set ourselves up for making mistakes and not executing skills to our full potential.

What you focus on affects how you feel in your body. What you focus on determines your self-confidence, your ability to stay calm under pressure, how you bounce back from mistakes and disappointments, your motivation level and your ability to handle adversity.

The good news is that you can train your brain to focus on you and your cheerleading, so you can execute your skills and routines with confidence and consistency!

It begins with AWARENESS.

The first step is to recognize when you are TIME TRAVELING with your thoughts. This means to notice when you start thinking about the past or the future.

> When you notice your time traveling thoughts, you can recognize your CHOICE POINT.

Your CHOICE POINT is an opportunity. Here, you can make a choice to continue thinking, or make a choice to bring yourself back into the NOW MOMENT to refocus on your skills!

We tend to spend a lot of time in our heads, so it can be challenging at first to begin to interrupt these thinking patterns and bring ourselves back to focus on the NOW MOMENT. It just takes some time, practice and patience!

INVITATION & PRACTICE

Today at practice: Build awareness of when you're time traveling and make a choice to come back to your NOW MOMENT. Notice your CHOICE POINT when your focus shifts to thinking, say "come back!" to yourself, and make the choice to quickly come back into the NOW MOMENT. Repeat when new thoughts come up.

Are you wondering what to focus on when you come back to the NOW MOMENT? Find your body in your physical space. Sense your feet connecting to the floor. Focus on the FEEL of the choreography and skills you are working on!

11

I create space for
REST and RECHARGE

Did you know that rest and recharge are essential aspects of your training that help you reach your maximum potential as a cheer athlete?

Many cheerleaders tell me they worry their coaches or parents will think they're being lazy if they ask for a day off or want some time on a weekend to just relax.

You're not being lazy when you rest! In fact, rest is doing something vitally important: You're giving the cells and particles in your body a chance to repair!

Think about it: How many more years would you like to continue doing cheer?

You need your body to last! REST is necessary for the long term strength and health of your body as a cheerleader.

If you're not getting enough rest and don't have enough space or time to repair from all the strain and repetition you put on your body, you become more prone to injuries, can't heal as quickly when you're hurt, and won't be able to execute the way you want to at practice and at meets.

It is time to create space for rest in your schedule today!

INVITATION & PRACTICE

Create Space: Look at your calendar and block off times daily this week to rest and pause. This can be as short as 5 minutes or as long as 30 minutes or an hour.

Sometimes you may feel like you don't have enough time to rest because you're so busy. But it's important to create this kind of space in your life so you have more energy and capacity to be doing ALL the things you want to be doing!

Reflect in your journal: What is it like to create space for rest?

12

I am calm and relaxed

Because cheerleading is a sport that can make you feel scared in your body, you need to be able to recognize what it feels like inside when your body is worried, AND have some go-to tools that settle your body down when it gets spooked.

You'll find it even more challenging to execute your skills if your body senses it might get hurt. You have automatic responses in your nervous system that come out to protect you, and those can interfere with you doing your skills well!

These automatic responses cause ACTIVATION in our bodies. ACTIVATION is how our bodies let us know we're frustrated, worried, scared, nervous, angry, and excited. If you're anticipating getting hurt, your muscles will tighten and your reaction time will slow.

When you're too ACTIVATED, you're not able to execute your skills and stunts cleanly or get your body to make the corrections your coach is giving you.

There are three ways your body communicates that it's ACTIVATED. You want to become aware of these and learn how they show up for you at practice or competitions, so you can support your body to calm down quickly.

Sensations in the body

Your body will give you physical cues that let you know it feels threatened. Examples: heart rate increases, breathing gets shallow, muscles get tight. You might notice you're running slower than normal, you can't get your body to go for your skill, or you're not able to make a correction your coach gives you. These are all signs that you are ACTIVATED.

Increase of thoughts

When our bodies are threatened, we get an increase of thinking, and most of the time it's negative! If you have an increase of your negative thinking and your CRITIC is out, this is a sign your body is ACTIVATED.

Images appear

Sometimes your imagination will send you images when your body is ACTIVATED. You might get a flash of the time you fell out of a stunt, dropped someone, or see yourself falling on your tumbling pass.

The more you can help your body feel safe regularly throughout practice, the easier it will be to get your body to do your skills when you feel stuck, implement a correction a coach is asking of you, and hit your routines with ease and confidence!

INVITATION & PRACTICE

Observation and Practice: Notice when you're ACTIVATED at practice today, then pause and use the 3-1-5 Breath (see below for directions) to help your body settle. On The Activation Scale, where 0 is your BASELINE and 10 is HIGHLY AC-TIVATED (worried, stressed, frustrated, nervous), notice when your number goes up on the scale and make a choice to pause and try this tool.

Check in with your body afterwards to see what your number changed to.

3-1-5 Breath: Take an inhale breath through your nose for 3 seconds, hold your breath for one second here in your chest, and then exhale down and out for 5 seconds. Make sure that your exhale time is longer than your inhale time.

A nice long exhale helps your body and nervous system calm down. You can try one breath at a time, or do this 3-5 breaths in a row. Notice the difference in your body after you use this tool.

Note with breathing and calming our bodies down: Sometimes when we're super ACTIVATED (your 0-10 scale number is high) and we bring a breathing tool in, if it doesn't calm us ALL the way down, we feel like it's not helping! When we're extremely ACTIVATED our body needs more TIME and PATIENCE to settle.

Instead of expecting an immediate result, try to notice the SMALL CHANGES in your body after you try a tool, like the 3-1-5 Breath.

For example, if you're a 9 when you notice you're ACTIVATED, do the 3-1-5 breath and notice how one breath brings you to a 7.5.

It's not all the way back to BASELINE, but it is headed in the right direction.

You may then decide to repeat the tool, or try something different to bring your number lower. Experiment here and see what works best for your body!

13

Curiosity is my default mode

Do you get easily frustrated with yourself at practice? Is a skill not going the way you want it to? Are you having trouble sticking your tumbling? Are you more tired than you want to be?

When things go wrong, it's important to remember to GET CURIOUS before you GET FURIOUS.

All too often cheerleaders report feeling especially frustrated with themselves at practice for a variety of reasons.

Whether it's for making a mistake, getting upset about not being able to get your body to go for a skill, or struggling to fix a correction from a coach, getting annoyed at yourself tends to be an automatic response for perfectionist cheerleaders.

Once you fall into the bad mood trap at practice, it tends to suck you down deep in a spiral of doom and gloom. It can be challenging to crawl your way out of this mood, which can wreck the rest of your practice and potentially the rest of your day!

When you're making mistakes or struggling to implement corrections, staying CURIOUS helps you figure out how to most effectively and efficiently solve the problem.

When your body is frustrated and tight, you can't think clearly or execute your skills as smoothly.

When you're CURIOUS, there's no pressure or judgement. There's no "right" or "wrong." You don't have to worry about being "good" or "bad." You get to NEUTRALLY OBSERVE what's happening.

Your body, as a result, stays calm and loose, because nothing "bad" is happening. You get to keep working on your skills!

Your frustration is INFORMATION for you. Pause and allow yourself to get CURIOUS about what to do differently.

When you get CURIOUS, you rebound quickly from mistakes and setbacks. You can execute corrections from your coach easily. You cheer your teammates on and are happy for them when they get new skills! Curiosity keeps you focused, motivated and engaged.

INVITATION & PRACTICE

At Practice: Set your main focus and intention today to GET CURIOUS during practice.

- What is your mood like when you hold this focus?
- How did your skills go?
- What felt different for you today?

Write down your observations after practice in your journal.

14

Overthinking is information

Cheerleaders and coaches sometimes believe that positive thinking is enough to get their bodies to do their skills when they're scared or frustrated.

You try telling yourself, "You can do it!" and "You got this!", but your body's still not letting you go for the skill. Then you think there's something wrong with you, which makes you feel super frustrated or down on yourself for not being able to do it.

You're NOT doing anything wrong here!

This is normal. Positive thinking isn't enough when it comes to our body doing its survival thing!

If your body's feeling fear, whether it's an actual threat or just a potential worry, there's no amount of positive thinking that can help. Your nervous system needs sensory information through embodiment practices that can communicate to your body there's no danger.

Excessive thinking in general, positive or negative, is a sign that your body is ACTIVATED and needs a tool to settle down.

Recognizing when you're overthinking at the gym, even when it's positive, is a good first step to refocus your attention and get your body where it needs to be to execute your skills with confidence: in the NOW MOMENT focused on FEEL.

INVITATION & PRACTICE

Observation and Practice: Today at practice, build awareness of when your thoughts are taking over your focus, make a choice to come back to your NOW MOMENT and use the Color Find Tool (described below) to settle your body.

Work on recognizing when your thoughts drift and make the choice to quickly refocus back into your NOW MOMENT. Repeat as new thoughts, positive or negative, come up.

Color Find Tool: Pick any color and begin looking around the gym. Find and name all the objects that you see with that color. Try to find 5-15 objects.

For example: Picking the color blue, I see a blue mat, a blue uniform, a blue bow, blue lettering on a sign, and blue in the sky out the window.

Notice how your body feels after you finish finding and naming objects. Refocus your attention on your skills.

15

My fear is normal

Cheerleaders tell me all the time that they think they're the only ones who get scared. They feel alone with their fear, like there's something wrong with them.

What?!

ALL CHEERLEADERS FEEL FEAR.

Why?

Well, cheer is scary! Fear is normal and a huge part of your sport.

As you progress through the levels, whether it's throwing a new skill, getting back up after a fall, or doing a stunt after you just watched your teammate get dropped, feeling fear is an integral part of being a cheerleader.

Because we're MAMMALS, our bodies have one main job: they are designed to keep us safe.

This means our body is constantly and automatically responding to the world around us and evaluating what it determines to be "safe" and what's "unsafe."

When the body experiences true danger, perceives there's potential danger, or remembers a time in the past when there was danger, it responds automatically, to gear up and protect us. Our heart rate increases, our breathing gets shallow, and our muscles get tight.

In cheer, you put yourself in experiences and situations regularly that your body interprets as "dangerous". However, by training and practicing over and over again, your body learns to feel comfortable doing these skills!

AND, when you're learning new skills in any arena of life, you make mistakes. In cheer, when you make a mistake, you can hurt your body. You might bash a leg, roll your ankle, or smash into the mat. The body remembers this!

Sometimes there will be an obvious reason for your hesitation or fear, like you just fell doing your front tuck step out and now feel scared to get back up and try it again. Other times, you may think you're fine, but your body has its own plan, like if you know you can do your standing back handspring, but you keep balking and your body won't let you go.

When you feel fear inside, or your body is not letting you go, it's simply information that your body doesn't feel "safe" at that moment, whether you think you "should" be scared or not.

The more you worry about being scared, or get mad at yourself for feeling fear or balking, the more you'll continue to struggle, feeling even more fear and stuckness in your body.

Instead, imagine getting super neutral about your fear in a way that allows your body to feel safe at practice.

What is neutral? Neutral means you don't have an opinion about your fear. You simply notice it's there and then use a tool to help your body settle down.

INVITATION & PRACTICE

Today at Practice: When you start to feel fear in your body or you're having trouble executing skills the way you'd like, pause and practice the Looking Around Tool.

Looking Around Tool: Feel your feet on the ground and let your head and neck scan the gym. Allow your eyes to land on one object. Describe this object neutrally (without any opinion) to yourself. Repeat with 2-5 more objects around the gym. Observe the small changes in your body after you finish describing the objects.

Now, go try your skill again and notice the changes.

- Do you feel less nervous inside?
- Was it easier to make your correction and perform the skill?

- Did you get your body to go?

If you still feel fearful after trying the Looking Around Tool, don't worry! That is good information. It means your body needs you to try the tool again.

Look around and describe more objects to yourself, noticing the small ways your body starts to feel calmer. Be patient with yourself and your body!

16

I easily let go of mistakes

When people learn new things we all make mistakes. It's a natural part of the learning process! In fact, you can't master anything without making mistakes. For example, when you're learning a new skill, you have to make hundreds of attempts before your body develops muscle memory to do it correctly consistently. This is totally normal!

All too often I hear cheerleaders talk about being mad at themselves for making any kinds of mistakes, as if they shouldn't have made them in the first place.

When you get mad at yourself for making a mistake, it keeps your body stuck feeling disappointed, embarrassed and frustrated.

When you get upset at yourself in these ways, your body automatically gets tight and activated, which further prevents you from executing your skills the way you want to. When you're not executing how you want, you get more frustrated, more tight, make even more mistakes and the cycle continues.

Instead, you can learn how to get neutral about your mistakes and let them go. The faster you let them go, the faster you can reset your mind and your body and refocus your attention on executing your skills.

INVITATION & PRACTICE

Today at practice: Every time you make a mistake, practice letting it go by using the Frustration Fists tool.

Frustration Fists Tool: When you make a mistake, pause and make a fist with each of your hands. Squeeze all of your irritation, frustration, and upset into your fists for 10-20 seconds. Say "let go" to yourself and as you do, slowly begin to relax your hands and open your fingers.

Sense into your wrists and forearms and notice how your shoulders soften. Refocus your attention on your routine or skill you're working on. Repeat as necessary.

17

I focus on me

Your biggest confidence drain to your performance is COMPARISON. When you compare yourself to a teammate or a competitor you are setting yourself up for failure. Instead, you want to stay focused on what YOU are dealing with and doing and not other people. All too often cheerleaders compare themselves to what and how others are doing, which distracts them from their own performance.

You want to stay away from comparing yourself to the athletes around you at practice, at competitions or on social media. If you spend time looking at other people and measuring yourself that way, it will wear down your confidence, make you feel badly about yourself and kill your motivation.

Too often I hear athletes say they're worried about falling behind their teammates. It's critical you learn to keep your focus on what YOU are doing: to stay centered, to stay inside yourself, and NOT on what others are doing or thinking. There is no behind. You have plenty of time.

Even more important: you don't want to compare yourself with how you used to be and then beat yourself up about how you're perceiving your progress. This is what cheerleaders have the tendency to do as perfectionists!

I see it all the time with athletes coming back from injuries or coming back to in-person training from a hiatus or time off. This causes unnecessary frustration and upset.

It is time to throw those past expectations out the window and focus on you and your present NOW MOMENT.

INVITATION & PRACTICE

Today at practice: Catch yourself when you find your thoughts drift to focusing on any people in your life, like your teammates, coaches, parents, or friends. Gently and kindly bring yourself back into your NOW MOMENT and focus on the FEEL of your skills.

Journal at home:

- What did you notice about your thoughts at practice?
- Who are you spending time thinking about?
- What was it like to redirect your focus back on YOU?

18

I trust myself and I trust my training

How long have you been participating in cheer?

How many years have you been in the gym?

How many hours a week do you train?

Sometimes as cheerleaders you forget you've been doing this sport for a long time! At a competition you might worry about little things or hyper-focus on all the things you want to make sure you don't forget to do in your routine. You try to cram in last minute corrections and changes. This takes away your focus on actually executing your routines in your NOW MOMENT.

You also forget you've been training with coaches who know what they're doing! They've prepared you in all the ways you need in order to execute cleanly.

You have practiced enough!
You have prepared yourself enough!
Your coach has coached you enough!

This is what you have been working so hard for.

Don't lose confidence because of a single mistake. Don't let a bad day at practice take your mind down a negative spiral of doomy and gloomy thoughts, where you feel defeated, like you will never reach your goals.

Instead, refocus. Today it's time to trust yourself and how hard you have been working at your goals!

INVITATION & PRACTICE

Practice Superperson Pose: This is a practice to create the imprint of confidence in your body, to EMBODY confidence. Stand in front of a mirror with your legs a little wider than hip distance apart. With your hands on your hips, raise your chest up in the air, reach your neck and head high and feel wide across your chest.

Ground down into the sturdiness of your feet and take 5-10 long, deliberate breaths here. Repeat daily leading up to a competition or when you want a confidence boost.

19

I shake it out and reset

In cheer (and in life!) many things happen that are completely out of our control.

Whether it's your coach being in a bad mood, the order of drills at practice, an early morning competition, or getting into an argument with your mom on the way to gym, situations come up that can grab your attention and distract you from the important stuff: the cheerleading!

I call these distractions UNCONTROLLABLES.

UNCONTROLLABLES are all the things that occur at practice or at competitions that we don't have control over, but we think about them anyway. They're often things you and your teammates stress out about together, like how mean a judge is at the competition, your coach's bad mood at practice, or whether you slept well the night before a big competition.

In fact, our brains tend to look for all the things that are going wrong, or aren't working, which can get us caught in a negative thinking spiral, tank our performance and influence our mood.

Have you ever had this happen? You know, the practice when you get switched out of your favorite stunt group and you spend all of your time bummed and upset, wishing you were back in the other group. The stunts your group is working on aren't hitting and you keep making mistakes. This makes you more frustrated with yourself, your coach and your teammates in the new stunt group.

When cheerleaders focus on UNCONTROL-LABLES, they upset their bodies, distract their minds and their skills suffer.

The more you get hooked into focusing on the UNCONTROLLBLES around you, the harder it can be to find the motivation and drive to work and train hard.

Because the mind and body are intricately connected, if you're spiraling in all of your negative thoughts, you can start to feel physically uncomfortable and 'out of sorts' in your body. This undermines your confidence and sabotages your performance.

UNCONTROLLABLES tend to be sneaky thoughts that steal us away from what we really need to be focusing on at practice or before or during a competition, which is the experience of what you are DOING: the stunts, skills and routines!

The faster you're able to identify when your attention is being pulled away to think about UNCONTROLLABLES, the faster you can regain control of your focus and redirect yourself back on your skills!

INVITATION & PRACTICE

Reflection: Start a list in your journal of all the UNCONTROLLABLES you tend to get caught focusing on at gym, competitions or in life. The more you're aware of what pulls your attention away from focusing on your cheerleading, the easier it will be to catch yourself when you drift to these UNCONTROLLABLES and reset!

Today at practice: Build awareness of when you start to think about UNCONTROLLABLES and make a choice to reset, with the Shake and Reset tool.

Shake and Reset Tool: When you notice you're caught up in your thoughts or your skills aren't going the way you want, make a choice to pause your body for a reset. Jump up and down and shake out your arms and legs for 30 seconds-1 minute.

Say to yourself in your head or out loud 'I reset my body'. Stop jumping or shaking and take a comfortable stance with your legs about hip distance apart. Sense your feet on the ground and the shift in your energy. Ask yourself, "What do I have control over right now?"

20

I see opportunity in the challenges

The sign of a real champion is revealed in how you handle the challenging times.

Anyone can feel confident and be positive when things are going great. It's easy to smile and feel motivated when it's all working out.

It's in those times when you feel frustrated, discouraged, hopeless and unsure that the seeds of true greatness reside.

How you react to and manage your failures, disappointments, performance slumps and plateaus willultimately determine whether you'll be a success or a failure in anything you attempt, in and out of the gym.

Life is not perfect. There is no way you can perform at 100%, 100% of the time. This is an unreasonable ask of your body.

You'll make mistakes. There will be moments of failure. You'll have a bad practice, or a bad meet. This is a given when you're on the journey of being a cheer athlete.

The only way to grow and improve as a cheerleader (or human!) is by making mistakes and failing.

Why?

Every time you come up short, you gain valuable information about what you did that didn't work. This helps you understand what you need to do differently next time for a better outcome.

It's how we RESPOND to challenges that determines our future success and the speed at which we recover from setbacks.

It's essential as you move through hard times, mistakes and setbacks, that you do everything in your power to respond to these challenges in as neutral or positive a way as possible.

INVITATION & PRACTICE

Research Reflection: Spend some time researching the career history of one or more of your favorite cheerleaders to learn about their journey: the failures or adversities they overcame and how they handled them.

Most athletes look at their idols in their sport and have no idea all the hardships they've faced in their career to get to their current level of success. Journal about what you discover.

21

My inspiration comes from within myself

Right in this NOW MOMENT, you never really know what and how much you can accomplish. Even if you're at the lowest point in your cheer career as you read this, flooded by self-doubts, surrounded by failure and floating in the unknown, you have the ability to do things you never imagined.

It's in these stressful times that you have an opportunity to get in touch with strengths and resilience you never knew you had.

Those qualities and gifts are there, underneath the doubts, the worries, and the fear. Your strengths and resilience live and breathe deep inside you.

It can feel hard to trust that, when things seem upside down.

Yet time and time again, we see evidence of perseverance and strength in the face of adversity.

So if you hang in there, if you stick it out, if you refuse to quit, if you keep working hard, then you could someday find yourself living your dream.

Your persistence and refusal to give up in the face of failure and the unknown are perhaps two of the most critical ingredients in your ultimate success. Winners become winners because they refuse to quit. They refuse to stop trying!

You have a choice in every moment how you respond. What do you choose right now?

INVITATION & PRACTICE

Activity: Make a WALL OF FAME in your room.

Create one wall in your room dedicated to your cheer dreams. Surround yourself with things that reflect your commitment to excellence, hard work and your goals. This can include posters or images of your favorite cheerleaders, motivational quotes or sayings, inspirational ideas, newspaper clippings, social media mentionings, medals and trophies.

Choose items and images that reflect your journey and successes. Put those front and center to remind yourself of everything you have accomplished!

22

My passion for cheer
fuels my motivation

───────────

Why do you cheer? Can you remember back to the moment when you first decided you loved being at the gym?

Was it doing your first handstand, forward roll or performing your routine with your team at your first competition?

When did you know cheer was something you wanted to be doing all the time?

Kids start cheerleading because it's FUN. SO MUCH FUN!

As you move up in levels or make the decision to compete and train competitively, cheer also becomes more serious and important. It takes hard work and intense dedication to be a cheerleader. In fact, you might even start to put FUN on the back burner.

Did you know when you're having FUN at practice and competition it improves your skills, execution and performance as a cheerleader?

When we have fun, our bodies stay loose and calm. When you're calm and relaxed, your body feels comfortable to execute the skills you've been working on so hard in training.

On the flip side, if you're NOT having fun and instead feel frustrated with yourself, worried about upcoming competitions or getting your skills, your heart rate increases, your breathing gets shallow and your body becomes TIGHT.

This isn't good news for your performance. You can't perform well if you're tight, timid or forcing things.

It's time to bring back the FUN in your cheerleading!

Keep an intention to
have fun EVERY DAY at practice.

You can work hard and still have a really good time! You get to have both.

If you notice you are not having fun, this is a perfect opportunity to shift your focus and your mood.

INVITATION & PRACTICE

Observe and Practice: Set the intention to have FUN at practice today! When you notice you're frustrated or not having FUN, use the Act As If tool.

Act As If Tool: ACT AS IF is a physical strategy you do with your body. It does NOT involve having to tell yourself anything. It's based on the principle that when you act the way that you want to feel, soon you'll begin to feel the way that you're acting. ACT AS IF is a bridge to take you from where you are NOW (feeling angry, frustrated, nervous, intimidated, unsure, tired) to where you want to be, (feeling in control, calm, confident, focused, having fun, energized).

When you notice you're not having fun, begin to ACT AS IF you're LOVING practice.

That is, you physically ACT AS IF you're having a blast, even though you can acknowledge that inside you're frustrated, tired, or freaking out. You walk confidently, keep your head up and start to embody what FUN feels like.

Write your observations in your journal after practice.

23

When I go slower, I arrive sooner

In cheer, sometimes slowing down is the way to meet your goals and expectations QUICKLY.

Sounds strange, right?

Patience is KEY.

This sport is hard on your body. Sometimes the body sends signals alerting us to slow down or ease off an injured body part. These signals show up as discomfort or pain.

As a cheerleader, you are tough! The cheer athletes I know are the best at shaking off those bumps, bashes, and aches and overriding their pain to keep pushing through and training.

Whether it's a coach saying "you're fine" or your Inner Coach saying, "it doesn't hurt that bad", oftentimes it's hard for cheerleaders to slow down, listen to their bodies and discern the difference between aching from the intensity of training OR from the beginning of an injury.

However, your body is designed to communicate when there is pain in order to prevent more serious injuries. Pain is information from the body that something is not right. Pain signals happen with increasing frequency and intensity when ignored so you don't continue to override these messages.

Especially if we're in and out of training due to circumstances out of our control, like moving, financial challenges, or recovering from an injury or illness, it's more necessary than ever to listen to our body so we make a safe and long lasting comeback.

One of the key things to keep in mind as you move forward after being out of the gym for any reason is this: the best way to regain your strength, flexibility, and skills is oftentimes the slowest way.

If you try to rush the process of coming back from a setback or injury by pushing and pressuring yourself to get your technique and stamina back, the only thing that's going to happen is amping up your nervous system and body. Rather than making up for lost time, you're going to end up getting frustrated, your muscles will tighten up, and they'll refuse to cooperate with you.

It's important to be smart about stepping back in. You need to listen to your body and stop if you're in pain.

The kinder, more patient, and more relaxed you are with yourself, the FASTER you will see healing and results.

When you're getting frustrated and angry, that's a sure sign you're pressuring yourself too much or you're pushing the envelope too hard and rushing. Learn to use those feelings (frustration, pressure and anger) as signs to slow down and take your time.

When we rush we make more mistakes and set ourselves back.

Instead, you want to pause, listen to your body, and be patient with yourself during your comeback in order to arrive sooner at your goals!

INVITATION & PRACTICE

Observation: Check in with your body multiple times at practice today.

Do you need a quick break? Go get some water or go to the bathroom.

Is there a body part that needs a rest? Let your coach know you're experiencing discomfort and need an alternative assignment.

Start to recognize when your body is sending you signals to slow down or stop and then practice advocating for yourself with your coach. Ask your parents or guardians to help you if you're nervous to speak up. Journal after practice about your observations and the way your body communicates to you.

24

My failures and mistakes are feedback.
They lead the way to my success!

All too often cheerleaders beat themselves up when they make a mistake or experience a failure.

But this won't inspire you to be a better cheerleader! Being hard on yourself does NOT motivate you to work harder.

In fact, it does the opposite:

Thinking in this way will sabotage your confidence and make you feel badly about yourself.

And, if you're thinking and feeling this way during a competition it will interfere with your confidence and ultimately affect your performance!

The only way to grow and improve as a cheerleader is to make mistakes. Failing, falling, getting blocks or having fear are NOT the problem. The real problem is how you respond to those situations!

You want to see failures and mistakes as neutral LEARNING opportunities. They do nothing more than point you in the direction of what you need to do differently.

For example, let's say you get a deduction off a routine at a competition because you fell out of your tumbling. You might get really upset with yourself, blame yourself for your team's score, and call yourself names, telling yourself you should've done it better. This only keeps you feeling down about yourself and distracts you when you move on.

Or, you can use this information to correct your mistake. You can make an effort to cleanly execute next time, staying in the now and focusing on feel. Your team score goes up because you hit your tumbling pass along with your teammates.

The more upset you get with yourself, the more it takes away from your training and your performance in the moment.

When you have a disappointing competition, or a frustrating practice, look at what you did wrong, and let it go! Do not get stuck focusing on it for days!

There is no way we can execute perfectly at 100%, 100% of the time. It is not humanly possible and cheerleaders are still HUMANS! (although you all do SUPER human stuff!)

How you respond to your mistakes matters.

The journey to your successes and dreams is always filled with mistakes, failures, doubts, fear, setbacks, blocks, upsets, illness, injury, and other uncontrollable circumstances. It's important to know they'll be there, so you're not surprised when they come up!

Start to recognize your mistakes and failures as an OPPORTUNITY to learn something new for next time!

INVITATION & PRACTICE

Observation and practice: Today at practice set the intention to let go of your mistakes or bad routines, using the Mistake Trash Can Tool to reset your focus.

Notice if you're feeling frustration, confusion, anger, hopelessness, self-doubt, sadness, or low confidence. All of these are signs you might be giving yourself a hard time and need to let it go. Journal after practice what you observed.

Mistake Trash Can Tool: Visualize there's a trash can close to where you're practicing. Use your imagination to picture the color, shape, and size. Every time you make a mistake, imagine throwing the mistake into the trash can, like a crumpled up piece of paper!

You can say to yourself, "let go" or "release now" (or something else that works for you) to support you in letting go of your mistake. Take an intentional breath after the mistake lands in the mistake trash can and refocus your attention on your skills. Repeat as necessary.

25

My mind and body
are in perfect alignment

What you think and say to yourself inside your head, whether you're aware of the thoughts or not, has a direct impact on how your body feels in the moment.

Science has proven the body can't tell the difference between something that's REAL from something we IMAGINE in our minds. Your brain and body are one big, integrated system.

This is what we mean by the MIND-BODY CONNECTION.

But what does this mean for you and your cheer skills?

What you think impacts how you feel inside your body. And how you feel inside your body influences how you perform.

Your MIND-BODY CONNECTION has a DIRECT effect on your performance.

To become a mentally strong cheerleader, you need to build AWARENESS about how your BODY works and how your MIND works, so you can get them aligned together to meet your goals with confidence!

Performance is self-fulfilling, which means you will always get what you expect!

When you think negatively, it makes you anxious, tightens your muscles, and speeds your breathing up. These can all lead to cold hands and feet, feeling antsy and jumpy, or hesitant and freezy.

These physiological changes always lead to slowed down mechanics, reflexes, slower foot speed, slower rotational speed in the air, fatigue and general bad performances.

If your outcome is not what you want, it's time to check in with your mind and body to see where the breakdown is happening.

If you're exhausted at the end of a practice and spiraling in negativity about how awful and hard conditioning is going to be, guess what? It's going to be extra CHALLENGING that day. You're going to feel even more tired and sore as you do your workout.

If you're worried you'll never get your new tumbling pass, and get super frustrated with yourself at practice as you work on things, guess what? You won't be able to execute that day. Your body will feel tight and clenched, making your skills impossible to achieve.

Fortunately, your MIND-BODY CONNECTION can also support your progress!

If you imagine yourself doing something well inside your mind's eye, your body will start to believe it to be possible!

When you practice visualizing yourself performing that upgrade skill in your imagination, you'll help your body feel comfortable going for it at gym.

When you visualize your most confident self executing your routine flawlessly, you create an imprint in your body. You're aligning your body and mind to believe and know you can do your routine and be confident at the same time. This will help you feel more confident the next time you're at a competition.

Begin observing yourself during your practices and competitions. Notice how your performance is a direct reflection of your thoughts in your head. Building awareness now about how these mind-body pieces align together is the first step in accessing your full potential as a cheerleader!

INVITATION & PRACTICE

Practice REFRAMING Strategy: Today after practice think of 5 things that happened that you weren't happy about and try to REFRAME them. That is, look for the positive in what happened at practice that you may have explained to yourself was negative.

For example, your coach just announced extra time working on standing tumbling today, where you're the most weak and scared. You begin freaking out, wishing you didn't go to practice today. The RE-FRAME in your reflection is that your coach set this practice up for exactly what YOU need to get stronger and improve as an athlete.

Write down in your journal the 5 things that happened to reflect on, and what your REFRAME is of the situation!

Practice: Today practice being a better Inner Coach to yourself in your life, both in and out of the gym. Use this as an opportunity to practice being kind to yourself, patient and flexible.

Pretend you're your own best friend. How would you talk to and support them? Being a good Inner Coach does not mean you have to try to 'think positively' and tell yourself you can do things.

Being a good coach means you're practicing patience with yourself regularly and being kind and understanding when things are scary, frustrating, hard or challenging.

26

I am confident!

The number one issue cheerleaders come talk to me about is CONFIDENCE: they all wish they had more of it!

As a cheer athlete, it's easier to do challenging skills and execute routines under pressure when you feel confident in yourself. It's like the missing secret layer to a cheerleader's ultimate success.

I know you want to have confidence in your skills, your competition ability, your work ethic, your routines, and your performance: all of the things!

Yet CONFIDENCE can feel like a far off place that's maybe even impossible to reach.

Guess what?

It's not!

You're always limited by what you believe is or isn't possible. If you believe you're not confident, I can guarantee you won't feel confident.

When you ARE confident, it FEELS a certain way in your body. You want this feeling to be a familiar place so you can access it when you're having moments of self-doubt.

Did you know you can perform to your ability and STILL have negative thinking and doubts going on in your head? Even champions navigate negative thinking. The trick is not getting caught up in your thoughts!

Here are some tips for an immediate confidence boost:

- Keep focusing on YOU and stop comparisons! Comparison will always make you feel worse and down on yourself. Cheerleaders who constantly compare themselves to their teammates and competitors will have very low self-confidence. Measure yourself against yourself and no one else!

- Let go of PERFECTIONISM. It will destroy your confidence.

- Celebrate your successes (big and small) EVERY DAY!

- Have a long term memory for your successes and short term memory for your failures.

- Stay neutral about your mistakes and failures. They're information for you. Learn from them and then let them go!

- Hang onto your winning moments and success stories! Write them all down in one place. Read them during moments of doubt.

INVITATION & PRACTICE

Visualization Practice: Develop a Confidence Cue: As you're going to bed, think about the last time you had a great competition. Remember all the things that went well and made the competition feel so amazing. Close your eyes and spend a few minutes replaying this impressive experience in your mind's eye, like a movie, where you can see, hear and feel what you did back then. Picture yourself at the location where the competition happened, hearing the shouts of encouragement from your teammates, hitting the pyramid perfectly, spotting your coach jumping for joy in the crowd, hitting zero, executing your routines confidently.

Once you've gone through the competition and routine/s, find one point in that competition, one particular moment or skill, that made you feel like it was a 'winning' experience. Focus on that one moment where you felt totally confident and like a champion!

Now, replay this one point in your mind's eye over and over again. Focus on all the emotions and sensations you experienced right then (confidence, excitement, joy, strength, lightness) and notice what you feel in your NOW MOMENT in your body.

Choose a word to represent this experience, which will be your Confidence Cue for training and competitions. This is a symbol, word or phrase that will remind you of those feelings of winning, confidence, courage, and strength. Your Peak Performance Cue can be:

- a WORD, like power or confidence
- a PHRASE, like '*I got this*' or '*Let's go!*'
- a COLOR like blue or purple
- an IMAGE, like a trophy or a tree

Bring this cue word to your practices to help recall these confident and winning feelings from your imagery!

27

I let go of my expectations!

———————————

The difference between your best and worst performances lies in your concentration and focus both before and during your routines.

The difference between having a productive, consistent and fun practice versus a challenging and frustrating practice is also determined by where you put your focus.

At competitions, cheerleaders who focus on the OUTCOMES they want or the EXPECTATIONS they have about their performance, won't get the results they're looking for.

During training, cheerleaders who hyperfocus on how they want the practice to go, the outcomes they really want, fixing a mistake or their expectations about getting a new skill, end up frustrated, forcing things or find themselves worried.

EXPECTATIONS are beliefs that you SHOULD or HAVE TO do something.

Imagine a cheerleader goes into their competition with the expectation of hitting everything in all of their routines, placing in the top 3 and beating a rival team.

These kinds of EXPECTATIONS make what they're doing too important.

EXPECTATIONS make your body tighten up physically. Your routines become SO important which leads you to trying too hard and forcing things, or being so fearful of making a mistake that you become paralyzed.

If you're overthinking before or during skills, you'll always perform badly.

The secret to performing
your best every time is
staying CALM and LOOSE!

The more you focus on your thinking, the more your reaction time is slowed in your routines and skills and your mechanics get wrecked.

Flexible goals can be helpful at practice to help fuel your motivation and desire for hard work, but they don't belong in competitions!

At a competition or practice, instead of focusing on your outcome expectations, bring in a mental toughness intention to focus on, like HAVING FUN or STAYING IN THE NOW MOMENT.

INVITATION & PRACTICE

Observation: Build awareness of when you start to think about the expectations you have for yourself on your skills and routines and make a choice to come back to your NOW MOMENT.

Work on recognizing when your thoughts drift to your expectations of yourself and make the choice to quickly refocus back into your NOW MOMENT. Repeat as you notice new expectations come up.

At your next competition: Do not bring your EXPECTATIONS into the competition. Go into this competition with the intention of HAVING FUN and staying in your NOW MOMENT. Let go of any expectations that surface. Reflect after the competition how this changes your mood and performance outcomes.

28

Getting out of my comfort zone is my ticket to peak performance

---

When you work hard towards your goals, there will be challenging moments and experiences that aren't always comfortable.

Part of embodying confidence is having the ability to GET COMFORTABLE BEING UNCOMFORT-ABLE.

So often I hear cheerleaders stressing out about their negative thinking, their lack of confidence, their fear, and their doubts.

When you're on the road to greatness and becoming a champion it's important to know this path is filled with uncomfortable feelings and thoughts. It's part of the process.

We all have these kinds of thoughts and fears. It's normal and to be expected!

The more we fear uncomfortable places or adversity, the MORE uncomfortable we feel when hard times show up.

Arguing with yourself about how you don't want to be uncomfortable or don't want to feel a certain way, will only get you more into your THINKING. This will impact your performance and training.

Instead, you want to neutrally observe your internal experience, acknowledge and give permission for those feelings to be there, and refocus on what is important.

If you want to become a champion, you have to take risks! This involves regularly stepping out of your comfort zone.

Your comfort zone is where you can do everything easily. Things in your comfort zone do not stretch you.

Being a champion involves pushing yourself!

Sometimes, you have to take ACTION before you feel motivated to step out of your comfort zone.

Taking small steps out of your comfort zone allows you to get used to these kinds of challenges. Your body will start to become familiar with this state of being and not fear it as much!

INVITATION & PRACTICE

At home: Put the saying GET COM-FORTABLE BEING UNCOMFORTABLE up in your room as a reminder to start getting comfortable with challenging yourself and give yourself permission to welcome any uncomfortable feelings that arise!

Reflection and Practice: Make a list of things that make you feel physically and emotionally uncomfortable at practice, that you avoid doing, but you know will make you a better cheerleader.

Challenge yourself at practice today by doing at least 2 of those things on your list that you think you can't do. Journal about what you observe when you push yourself out of your comfort zone.

29

If it is to be, it's up to me!

Cheerleading is HARD WORK. You can't become a successful cheerleader without putting in time and effort for your physical training!

AND

You make many additional sacrifices when you decide to become a cheerleader.

Your free time gets limited. Your priorities are different from other kids your age. Your weekends are filled with travel, training and competitions.

As a competitive cheer athlete, there are CHOICES you make on a day to day basis that affect your performance at the gym and during competitions. From the food you eat, to the bedtime you keep, to your effort during conditioning when your coach isn't watching, your dreams and goals are fueled by your choices.

Sometimes these choices aren't easy. You may want to go to a party the night before a competition, but make the decision to stay home and go to bed early. This choice supports your bigger dream of becoming a champion.

You're in control of the choices you make. You have the strength, grit, and determination to keep putting in the work necessary to meet your goals and follow your dreams. Your cheer success is dependent on your self awareness in and out of the gym, so you can make choices that support you reaching your goals!

INVITATION & PRACTICE

Reflection: What is your long term goal in cheer? Name it, speak it, write it, and put it up proudly in your room!

Reflection: How is what I'm doing TODAY going to help me get to my BIG Goal? Take this question with you to practice each day! When you are bored, tired, scared, or struggling at practice, take it out and ask yourself, "How is what I'm doing right now going to help me get to my goal?"

Journal about what you notice at practice today when you hold this reflection.

30

I am grateful

What are you grateful for today?

There are so many amazing things unfolding around you, supporting you all of the time. Did you know that? We tend to take these things for granted or don't even recognize they're happening in the first place.

The EARTH is supporting your ability to breathe and survive on the planet. We live on an ALIVE, giant green floating rock in the middle of space.

Your BODY works so hard for you, often completely out of your awareness and you don't have to effort to make anything happen. Your internal body systems function automatically. They make sure you're breathing, digesting food and communicating coherently. These systems allow you to hold your body upright, walk, run, chew, hear sounds, perceive danger, admire beauty, and so much more!

Your body's design is AMAZING. It's working all the time at the gym for you, allowing you to create new embodiment patterns, as you train your body to learn all of your skills and put together routines.

Even on the crummiest of days, there's so much to be grateful for!

Gratitude is our greatest strength. It helps put our challenges into perspective.

When you feel gratitude for something, it creates a certain energy, which makes you feel good in your brain and throughout your physical body.

It's not just about thinking how grateful you are for someone or about something. It's about experiencing the sensations of gratitude in your body. What does it feel like for you?

When we spend time in this state of gratitude, our body is flooded with this supportive and energizing vibration. This promotes motivation, good moods, and assists us to truly embody confidence.

The more we can help ourselves focus on embodying these kinds of feeling states, like GRATITUDE, JOY and LOVE, the better we feel overall in our life.

The better you feel inside yourself and about yourself at practice, the more confidently, fearlessly and effortlessly you will execute your skills and hit all of your routines!

INVITATION & PRACTICE

Journal Practice: Choose one or both

Evening Gratitude Reflection: Before you go to bed spend a few minutes reflecting on your day and write down 5 things you're grateful for in your life or in cheer. Do this for one night, or commit to this practice for a week.

Notice how your mood shifts if you participate for multiple nights in a row.

Morning Gratitude Reflection: Start your day with a Gratitude Reflection and write down five things that you are grateful for in your life or cheer. Do this for one morning or commit to this practice for a week.

Notice how your day shifts if you participate multiple days in a row.

Acknowledgments

I am forever grateful to my father, Dr. Alan Goldberg, for my initiation into the field of peak performance and for over 10 years of mentoring. Much of how I look at performance potential and navigating blocks and fears in my work with athletes stems directly from the foundational pillar of studying with him, along with learning from all of his brilliant books and audio programs for athletes, coaches and parents. He is a true pioneer in the field and I am honored to continue to bring his legacy and frameworks to more athletes, coaches and parents.

Additionally, I want to acknowledge and express my gratitude for Tayla Vexler Nessbit, the owner of Hampshire Gymnastics in Amherst Massachusetts, her staff and amazing gymnasts! It is my time with the team for over 3.5 years which initially fueled my love of helping gymnasts, cheerleaders and coaches navigate fear, blocks and access their confidence and potential!

I want to honor Peter Levine and his pivotal work of Somatic Experiencing®. This modality informs all layers of my work and is the lens through which I examine and work with performance problems.

I want to acknowledge and express my gratitude for Sue Hitzmann, manual therapist and creator of the MELT Method®. At my first training she said, "You don't cause pain to get out of pain" and that has stuck with me as I educate and support athletes in their repair and recovery processes. As both a MELT Instructor and student, I experienced the extreme healing benefits of this revolutionary self care method in my own body. The MELT Method is a vital resource in my work with athletes to help them expand their body awareness, support pain free training, facilitate healing, and provide an easy hands on tool to promote nervous system health.

So much gratitude to my book coach, Leah Kent, for her stellar organization, cheerleading and magickal supportive space for my vision.

Of course this acknowledgement section would not be complete without mentioning my beautiful husband and two vibrant boys. Without their patience and support and many days of letting "daddy" run the show, this book and bringing my work into the world would not be possible.

Resources

For more peak performance resources, books and audio programs visit **competitivedge.com**

For injury prevention, rehabilitation care, decreasing risk of repetitive stress on the body and helping rebalance the nervous system visit: **meltmethod.com**

Stay Connected

To connect with Sara for private session work with athletes, consultations for coaches and parents, or to book Sara for a clinic, workshop or speaking engagement, please visit:

peakperformwithsara.com and **saravatore.com**
or send an email to **sara@saravatore.com**

To download additional resources to support you with your peak performance mindset and embodiment practices visit:

peakperformwithsara.com/cheerbook-resources

Cheer Glossary

ACTIVATION

Activation is an automatic response our body physiology moves into when the body is sensing any kind of 'danger' or is responding to the environment. We perceive three different kinds of danger: actual danger, perception of danger and memory of danger. When we encounter any of these, automatic programs in our body kick on to help us react or respond. These physical responses can feel like a racing heart, shallow breathing, or tightening muscles.

ACTIVATION is how our bodies let us know we're frustrated, worried, scared, nervous, angry, or excited.

When you're too ACTIVATED, you're unable to execute your skills and stunts cleanly or get your body to make the corrections your coach is giving you.

BASELINE

Your BASELINE is your foundational neutral zone in your body. It's the resting place for your body and your state of being (how your body feels) when you're grounded, connected, centered, and present.

CHOICE POINT

Your CHOICE POINT is the moment your awareness recognizes you got distracted from your NOW MOMENT. It's also a moment of opportunity for a cheerleader. It's when you have the awareness that something is not going the way you want. You might notice you're caught in your thoughts, you're getting frustrated, or you just can't seem to make a correction and are getting upset with yourself.

Your awareness of this choice point provides the opportunity to quickly bring yourself back into the NOW MOMENT to refocus on your skills!

EMBODIMENT

EMBODIMENT is your self-perception of BEING in your own body.

Being able to SENSE your body, to feel your body connected in your environment, and also to be able to identify internally what is happening inside your body (for example, your heart beat, breath or tightening muscles).

FELT-SENSE

FELT-SENSE is your awareness of your internal body sensation experience and your perception of locating your body in the space and environment you are in.

FOCUS ON FEEL

FOCUS ON FEEL is sensing your body doing your skills in your NOW MOMENT instead of focusing on your thoughts. When you focus on feel, you can focus on the shapes that your body is making as you do your skills and stunts.

MAMMAL

Mammals are warm blooded animals and are governed by their biological drive to survive. Humans are mammals and as a cheerleader and a mammal, your body's main priority is to keep you safe.

NERVOUS SYSTEM

The nervous system is like a super highway of communication for your body. It's the wiring that works automatically to keep your body functioning, surviving and thriving. It's what allows your body to breathe and enables all the other systems to work.

NEUTRAL OBSERVER

Your NEUTRAL OBSERVER is the part of you that is able to witness what's happening inside of you (your thoughts, sensations, and feelings) and what is happening around you (the environment, other people) without JUDGEMENT or an OPINION.

NOW MOMENT

The NOW MOMENT is when your attention is on what your body is DOING in the present time.

You do your best cheerleading when you are in your NOW MOMENT. This is where you're sensing your body DOING the stunt, tumbling and each skill. You're focused on the FEEL of your body in the shapes.

SELF AWARENESS

Self awareness is your perception of YOU. Awareness of YOU: what is happening in YOUR mind, in YOUR body, and in the environment around YOU. When we have awareness of what is happening, then we have choice. Self awareness is the key to change.

SENSATIONS

The SENSATIONS are your internal experiences inside your body, like your heartbeat, muscle twitching or butterflies in your stomach.

Sensations give us information about what our body needs and what our truth is in the moment.

Some examples of sensations:

Calm, warm, heavy, jittery, tense, frozen, stuck, clammy, hot, sparkly, light, long, hollow

UNCONTROLLABLES

Uncontrollables are all the things that happen externally in your environment that you don't have control over.

Some examples of uncontrollables:

- what mood your coach is in at practice

- how good your competitors are

- how well you slept the night before a big competition

- your teammates performance in the routine

About the Author

Sara Vatore, M.Ed., SEP, is a Peak Performance Coach, Somatic Experiencing® Practitioner and MELT Method® Instructor. Sara synthesizes and uses breakthrough techniques in the field of peak performance to help athletes understand where they are stuck and how to turn it all around.

She works privately and in groups with athletes of all ages, leaders, entrepreneurs, parents and coaches to support them in navigating fears and blocks to access and embody their full potential. Sara understands the importance of looking at the brain-body connection as a whole system and its direct effect on peak performance.

Sara is on a mission to educate coaches, parents and athletes about the importance of rest and restore as the missing piece for reaching ultimate peak performance through nervous system regulation and connective tissue care. She works with athletes and teams to integrate the MELT Method® into their weekly training programs to get the most out of repetitive training, reduce damage to the body, minimize the risk of injury, and speed up recovery time.

With over 16 years of experience working with kids and their families, including a background in school guidance counseling, Sara has a deep understanding of family and system dynamics, children, adolescents and human development.

She lives in Western Massachusetts with her husband and two boys, loves to dance, and spends all her free time in nature.

To learn more about Sara and her services, please visit:

saravatore.com
peakperformwithsara.com